MERCEDES -BENZ

Front endpaper
Magnificent example of the 500K tourer of 1934. Its engine is a supercharged 5-liter straight-eight. This 500K is one of the few to have right-hand drive

(below)
A 450SLC fixed-head coupé of 1974

MERCEDES-BENZ

Stuart Bladon

Supercharged Mercedes-Benz S sports
two-seater of 1927 had a six cylinder
6.8-liter engine developing 180 bhp

Contents

INTRODUCTION

Daimler and Benz are the names of the great founders of the company which still trades, nearly a hundred years later, with the same ideals of producing the best cars possible. But where does Mercedes come into it?

It was in 1882 that one of the two founders, Gottlieb Daimler, moved to Bad Canstatt, then a flourishing spa, but now a suburb of Stuttgart, and started to work in a conservatory-workshop in the grounds of his home, to improve the four-stroke engine which Nikolaus Otto had invented – hence the Otto cycle. He was helped by Wilhelm Maybach.

Daimler's early achievement (in 1883) was the inventio of 'hot tube ignition', a tube protruding through the cylinde wall, and heated by the exhaust gases, to ignite the fuel/a mixture. From this was derived the word *chauffeur,* bein the name given (after the French word *chaud,* meaning heat) to the man who warmed up the ignition tubes for hi master in the morning when the engine was cold.

Nineteenth-century milestones

In 1885, the first form of car actually ran, when a wooden-framed vehicle with this engine chugged throug

park of Daimler's villa on 10 November. It was more a
n of motorcycle than a car, since the two main wheels
re in line, and two small ones on outriggers at the side.

e first four wheelers

ear later came the first true four-wheel car, when
mler installed one of his engines in a specially ordered
riage without horse shafts. In the same year of 1886,
Benz of Mannheim lodged his significant patent for 'a
icle operated by a gas engine… whose gas is
erated from vaporizable substances by an apparatus
ried on the vehicle'.

Karl Benz and Gottlieb Daimler worked separately. Each
ned his own business to promote his inventions and the
elopment of the automobile and, a remarkable fact,
y never met, although they lived only about 60 miles
n each other.

Daimler-Benz was formed from the merger
of the two separate companies founded by
Gottlieb Daimler and Karl Benz. Water
cooling was used for Benz's first car (below,
right); Daimler's first machine (bottom) was a
form of motor cycle with outriggers. The
Mercedes name was used by Daimler from
1900; (below, left), a splendidly preserved
1904 example

The first Mercedes

An enthusiast for the cars which Daimler produced was the Austrian businessman and consul-general Emil Jellinek, who lived in Nice. He went to Canstatt, saw Daimler, and ordered considerable numbers of his cars, which he sold among wealthy friends and acquaintances on the French riviera.

In 1899, Jellinek entered a 23 hp Daimler in the touring competition of Nice, and used a pseudonym – Mercédès. It was the name of his pretty ten-year-old daughter. The car won first prize, and when in the following year he ordered 36 of Daimler's latest design, he suggested that the name Mercedes be used for them. It is a Spanish girl's name, and the word means 'mercy'. It was registered as the trade name for the Daimler car in 1902.

Daimler died in 1900, and his two sons carried on the business; it was on their suggestion that both three- and four-pointed stars were adopted as trademarks, but only the three-pointed star was used.

Daimler-Benz is born

In the depression and roaring inflation of 1924 in German automobile manufacturers had difficulty in staying in business. The merger of the then well-established firms of Benz and Daimler was a logical move to ensure survival.

From Benz came the laurel wreath, which had been adopted in 1909 as the company's trademark, replacing the gear wheel which had previously been used. From Daimler came the name Mercedes, which had persisted as the name for all the company's cars. Thus came the extraordinary situation which continues, and no doubt will go on as long as cars survive, that the company Daimler-Benz builds the car called Mercedes-Benz.

This Daimler (right) is generally accepted as the world's first four-wheel car. At Daytona Bay, Florida, the famous Blitzen Benz (below, centre) with Bob Burman covered the flying mile at a record average speed of 141.7 mph. Early beginnings: the 1894 Benz 1½ hp Velo (bottom, right), and (below) a Daimler Mercedes of 1913

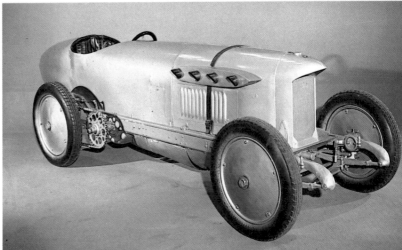

Mercedes script on the radiator and the famous three-pointed star date back to 1909. This six-cylinder 7-liter Mercedes of 1924 was known as the Targa Florio

Four-seater Mercedes touring car of 1902-4 (below) is the Mercedes Simplex. (Lower picture): Huge headlamp of a 1904 Mercedes 70 hp. After the 1926 merger of Daimler and Benz, the cars became known as the Mercedes-Benz. 1927 model (right) has twin stars on the radiator shell, as well as the now famous free-standing mascot

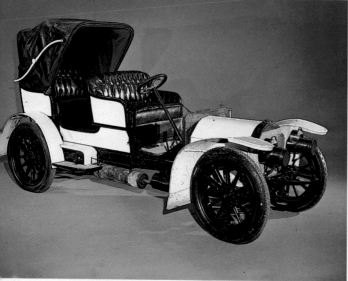

Luxury image of the ocean-going liner was appropriately used in Mercedes advertising. An early (1923) six-cylinder supercharged two-seater (top) contrasts with the later (1932) SSK tourer (left)

Introduced in 1927, the supercharged S had a 6.8-liter six-cylinder engine, and led to this 1929 model, the 38/250 TT

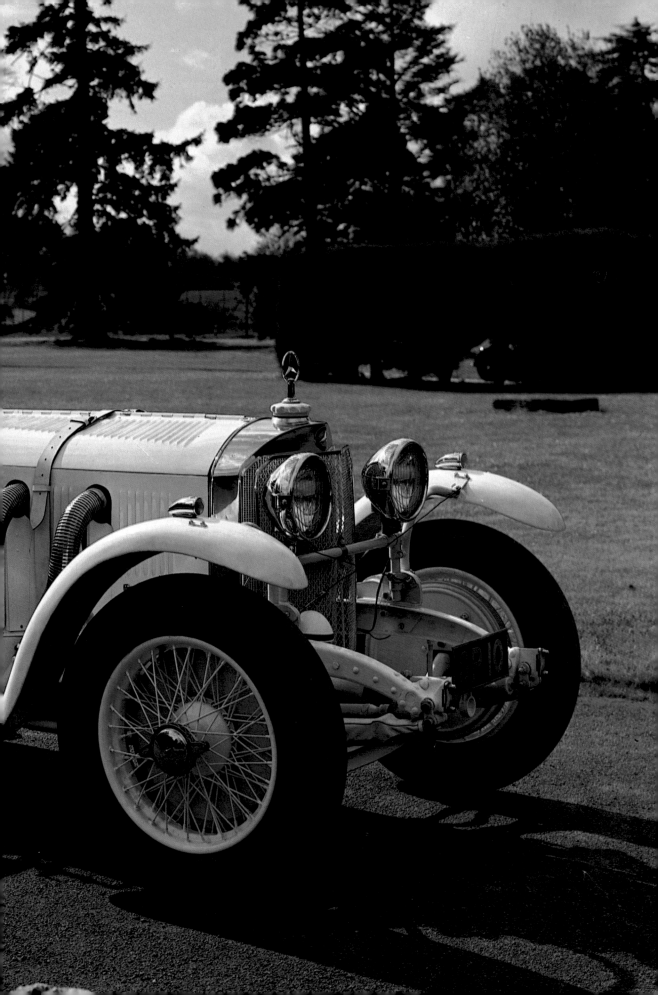

1929 7.2-liter supercharged two-seater
(above), and (left) an unusual Mercedes –
the mid-engined four-cylinder two-seater
sports of 1934. One of the series of "bread
and butter" saloons of the 1930s is seen (far
left), a 1936 Mercedes-Benz 200

BEHIND THE THREE POINTED STAR

Many people would like to own a Mercedes-Benz, even if they have never driven one and can only imagine what it would be like. Such is the strength of the image the company has developed for itself that perfection is presumed, and taken for granted. Centerpiece of the legend behind the oldest car make in existence is the three-pointed star symbol which graces every model.

On saloons, it stands as a mascot – spring-loaded so that it would not add to the injuries of anyone hit by the car in an accident – and the light glints on its triangular-section arms; on the sports cars it is enlarged, and forms the centerpiece of the grille.

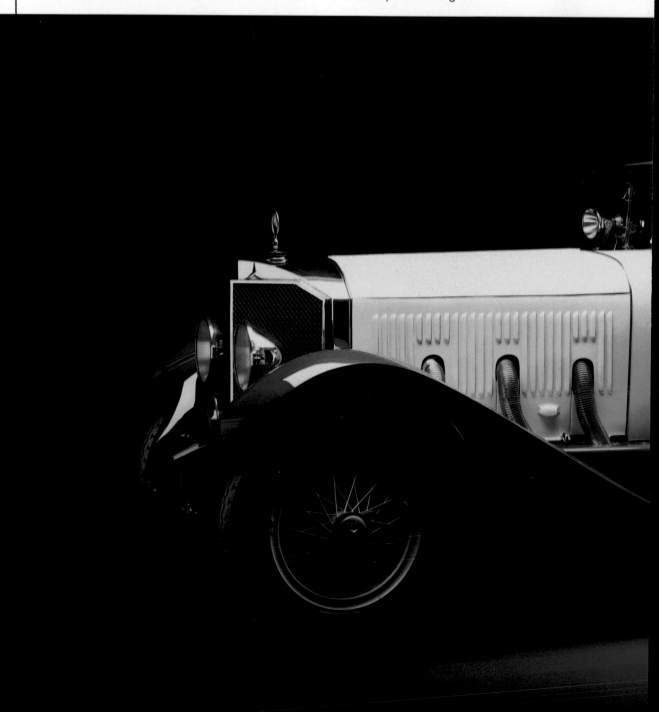

A legend of quality

Strength, reliability, solidity and lasting service, these are the implications of the Mercedes legend; they are the attributes which the Mercedes buyer expects to find, and for which he is prepared to pay generally much higher prices than are asked for rivals of similar size and performance. The buyer is seldom disappointed.

Balance of design, advanced technology and the optimum combination of safety, quality, durability and economy are the basic principles of a successful model policy, say Daimler-Benz. All of these aspects have been, and always will be, the subject of intense research to retain the strengths on which the company has been built up over the years. The quality is evident in the way in which the cars last, and is endorsed by the extensive use of Mercedes saloons for taxi work in so many countries around the world.

Nearly half a billion dollars are spent on research every year. In particular, the Mercedes-Benz car has an unquestioned reputation for safety, won by costly perseverance in crash-testing, accident investigation and research into, for example, seat belts which self-tension in event of an accident, and into development of the chassis for the safest possible handling behavior in an emergency on slippery roads.

Six-cylinder Type 28/95 of 1926, with four-door tourer bodywork. Engine capacity was 7,273 c.c.

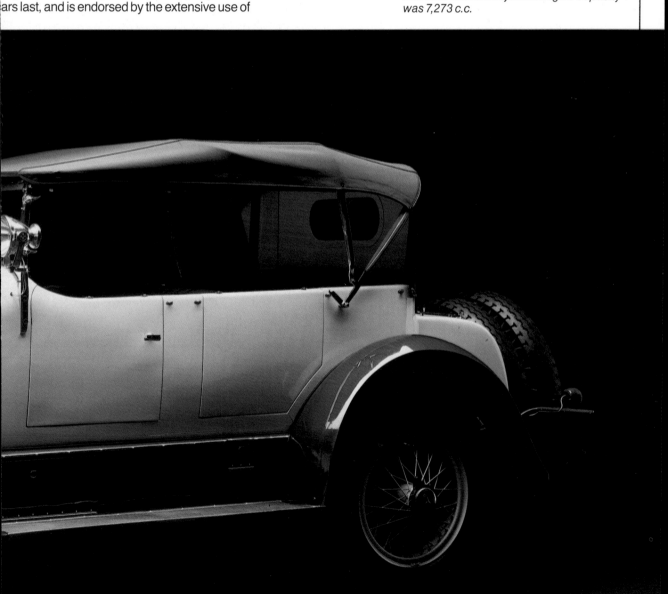

Manufacture and export

More than 12 per cent of all cars built in Germany are Mercedes products. Yet the company's strength is partly owed to its long policy of developing overseas markets. Almost half of the cars built, and well over half of the trucks, are exported, and they go to a 170 different countries. West Europe, North America and the Middle East are the company's chief markets. The company has its own marketing operation in the important export countries.

In an inter-linked production system, Mercedes products are built at 11 factories in Germany. Main assembly is carried out at the two big plants at Stuttgart. One is at the traditional headquarters of the company, called Stuttgart-Unterturkheim, the other at nearby Sindelfingen. Increasing numbers of Mercedes cars are also now being built at the recently rebuilt plant at Bremen in the north of Germany, former home of the once-renowned Borgward make. Other plants produce components, such as the one at Düsseldorf which makes steering assemblies.

Outside Germany there are a number of other Mercedes production works and assembly plants, and

ortant subsidiaries in the United States, Brazil,
entina and Spain. Around the world, Daimler-Benz
ploys some 185,000 people.

ery special sort of car

e a typical day at the Sindelfingen plant, and you find
wards of 1500 people at a reception center at the factory.
ere's a holiday atmosphere, and wives and children are
ng about. What is going on? you may ask. As happens
ost every working day, between 500 and 600 brand

new Mercedes are being taken away by their new owners.
Not for them the usual routine of train shipment and
onward travel by delivery driver. If the new car is going to be
a Merc, you go out here to take delivery in person, if you
can possibly spare the time. It's that sort of car.

*Post-war elegance of style in the 300
Automatic with fuel injection for its 180 bhp
engine, new at the London Show in 1957*

Famous star, and the laurel wreath emblem inherited from Benz & Cie (far left); 300S four-door convertible (left). Diesels have long been an important part of Mercedes production, and the picture (left corner) shows three generations of diesels: from left of picture, 260D of 1936, 170D of 1949-53, and 200D. (Below): The exciting 300SL of 1956 (see next chapter)

Overleaf: car of the legend: the 300SL "gull wing"

A particular favorite: the 230SL launched in 1963 (top); its successor was the broader V8-powered 350SL (above). A V8 engine of 4,520 c.c. capacity powered the 450SE (left)

*Traditional radiator surround and mascot
continue on the coupé of 1964 (centre, right).
On its left is one of the first generation
S-Class models (280S, 280SE and 350SE),
and (far right) the 500SLC of 1982. Derived
from the second generation S-Class was the
two-door SEC coupé of 1984, available with
3.8- or 5-liter V8 engine (below)*

Popular Mercedes (top): the Type W123, with
engines from 2-liter to 2.8-liter. (Below): Not
the usual terrain for a Mercedes, but this is
the 280GE Geländewagen (cross-country
car). Choice of engines for the two-door
coupé was 2.3-liter four-cylinder – called
230CE (right) – or 2.8-liter six-cylinder
(280CE). Smaller saloon launched
1982, the 190 (above)

THE LIGHTWEIGHT SPORTS CAR

Although the Mercedes-Benz empire has been built on a marvelous reputation for worth, solidity and longevity, the marque has also consistently been a driver's car. Driver appeal has been exemplified in the sports cars that have backed up the ordinary models of the range. For the past 30 years, they have been given the identity letters 'SL'.

In German the words *Sport Leicht* were used to ider the first of the series – a full translation might be 'the lightweight sports car'. The figures 300 indicated the approximate engine size, as the 300SL which appeared original racing form in 1952 had a 3-liter six-cylinder engine.

The first SL

On the market early in 1954, the first SL was derived from the car produced to take Daimler-Benz back into motor racing in 1952. The road-going version was again impressively fast, with a top speed of 129 mph, and it would accelerate through the gears to 100 mph in what was then the very quick time of 21.0 seconds.

The six-cylinder engine was unusual in being inclined over to its left side – a layout used by many manufacturers now but rare in the 1950s. Such a layout was made easier by the use of fuel injection instead of carburettors; and that, too, was unusual then among lesser makes, but almost a hallmark of the Mercedes engine.

The most remarkable feature of this first SL was the use of top-hinged doors for its coupé body. Seen from the rear, the 300SL with both doors open looked reminiscent of a seagull in flight, and this earned for the SL the nickname Gull Wing. When you opened its heavily curved door upwards, you were confronted with a huge width of sill, and quite an athletic movement was necessary to clamber inside. But things were made easier for the driver by a clever arrangement for the steering wheel to pivot almost to the horizontal, making it easier to get the legs in underneath it.

Much the same body but with much less power was introduced later, having a four-cylinder engine instead of the 3 liter six. Capacity was 1897 cc, and like the 300SL it

Racing version of the SL, the 300SLR won the 1955 Mille Miglia (left). Reason for the "gull wing" name revealed in views of the 300SL (below)

had single overhead camshaft valve gear. Some people decried this model, called the 190SL, and said it was too under-powered; but that disappointment was probably in contrast to the enormous performance of the 300SL.

A bad feature of these and other contemporary Mercedes cars was the rear suspension design. It used an arrangement known as the 'swinging axle', which caused the rear wheels to change their camber angle on bumps and in hard cornering, which upset the handling. In the right hands they could be controlled, as many racing drivers demonstrated, but the inexperienced driver could be caught out by the resultant oversteer on corners.

The refined sports car

'If it's acceptable for the sports saloon, then why not for the sports car as well?' people asked when they noted with surprise the decision of Daimler-Benz to offer power assisted steering for the new 230SL that was launched in 1963. This new model marked a tremendous advance from the former 190 and 300SLs, although there was no attempt at first to match the 300SL's performance. The 230SL – so named because of its 2.3 liter engine (an overhead camshaft six again) – brought refinement and comfort to the open sports car.

Its hood fitted neatly, and there were frameless glass

dows. When folded back, the hood disappeared [all] covered by a hinged panel. The car was a delight [e]specially when good weather made it possible to [put] hood down. Especially in automatic transmission [the] 280SL tended to be under-geared and fussy at [b]ut there were few other faults. Owners could fit a [tai]lored hard-top for the winter. Further refinement [th]e power followed, with the introduction of the wider, [and] still more comfortable 350SL in 1971. Just as [S]L range had been extended by choice of 2.5 or [en]gines, so the 350SL became available later with [a slen]der 2.8 liter engine, again called the 280SL in [th]e body change. The choice widened, with arrival of the 4½ liter V8 engine (450SL), and the 350 became the 380SL.

Then came the current contender for the title of the most exciting sports Mercedes of all, the 500SL. It has a V8 5 liter engine, and ranks high among the world's top sports cars. It's no longer very *leicht*, but still very much a sports car.

300SL Roadster of 1957 (left). *A 300SL coupé* (below), *and* (lower) *the racing version, 300SLR*

Rare collection of three 300SLs (above). (Far left and below): Two more well-preserved examples of the coveted 300SL. Power unit was a 3-liter ohc six-cylinder engine with Bosch fuel injection, and the engine was inclined to the left of the car to keep the bonnet height down

Overleaf: A 1981 Coupé version of the SL – a 1981 380SLC

Inviting interior of the 300SL (top, left); the steering wheel could be tilted for easier access. As well as the gull wing door model, there was a convertible 300SL (far left). Two-seater convertible of 1982 (left) came with choice of 2.8-, 3.8- or 5-liter engine. (Above): 300SL of 1957 with the "third generation" SL – the 450SL launched at Geneva in 1973

Fixed-head version of the SL two-seater, the
350SLC (left). Luxury interior of a 1977
450SL (above, top), and the most desirable
of all the later SLs – the V8 5-liter 500SL
(above)

THE STAR OF LUXURY

Over the years, the Mercedes has always been a relatively expensive car – something to buy as an investment in quality and durability rather than for sheer good value. At the luxury end of the range, there have always been models in the Mercedes line-up to satisfy the most discerning tastes, and to sell to people of great personal wealth or to those with company backing to meet the high investment cost. The Mercedes vies with Rolls-Royce as the natural choice for company chairmen, heads of state and the very rich.

In addition, many Mercedes models have been converted to meet special luxury needs or to be distinctiv

often most extravagant ways. The demand for special Mercedes-Benz bodywork and interior embellishments developed to such extent in the late 1970s and '80s that it has been sufficient to be the main source of livelihood for a number of British bodywork specialists.

Custom conversions

Daimler-Benz have always been very reserved about work of this kind. They know it is too important a market for it to be ignored, yet they are wary of suffering claims of dubious reliability as a result of improperly researched modification of their products. When they are asked to approve a conversion, the usual policy is to test and examine and then, when really satisfied that the work done matches their own standards, they declare that they 'will not forbid their dealers to handle it'. This is about as near as they would ever get to giving official factory approval for major conversion work.

British companies have established a flourishing business with the Middle East, where there is great enthusiasm for luxury cars, a desire to have something distinctive and better than any other; sometimes the most fabulously expensive adaptations have been commissioned.

One of the successful conversions was the ingenious extension of the body of the Mercedes 500SEL to turn it into a limousine. Design was by Le Marquis in the U.K.

Known as the Grosser, the huge 600 was powered by a 6.3-liter V8 engine. The Mercedes star has always been a symbol of quality and luxury

and conversion was undertaken by Tickford of Milton Keynes, a division of Aston Martin.

This conversion is particularly clever for the way in which standard parts are used. A new center pillar is welded in position to the rear of the original one, and a new door is made up each side, using the front part of a rear door and the back part of a front door. This means using the framework of two doors just to make one central door each side, but if you sketch it out on a piece of paper you soon see why this is necessary: the new central door has to mate with the differently shaped fore and aft pillars.

The limousine is offered as a six-door, or the more popular arrangement is that the center door has no exterior handle, and is intended to remain closed for all time. It would not provide very good access to the rear compartment because of the intrusion of the center bulkhead and division, which usually houses television and video.

A world of comfort

Other luxury fittings include a refrigerated drinks cabinet, the most extravagant hifi radio and cassette units with multiple speakers and graphic equalizers, radio telephone, and intercom to communicate with the driver. One special Mercedes conversion even had a multiple drinks dispenser allowing rear compartment occupants to dial whatever instant drink they required.

Of special note is the work done by Duchatalet, which has featured at a number of the international motor shows. This consists of magnificent embellishment of Mercedes 500s with the most lavish interior materials, special external decor including gold plating, and the incorporation of every conceivable extra.

The variety of orders is so complex that it needs many individual firms to tackle them. It is small wonder that Daimler-Benz are happy to leave this side of the business to the specialists, including another branch of conversion work in strong demand for some countries – bulletproofing.

Although Daimler-Benz now finish the range with the standard long-wheelbase saloon version of the 5 liter saloon, the 500SEL, at one time they produced a huge limousine of their own, the 600. It came in two sizes and was called the Grosse (large). It had only four doors, with central separation and division, and under the bonnet was a huge V8 engine of 6.3 liter capacity.

In place of the huge 600, a less spectacular but still very impressive limousine continues in production at the time of writing, the long-wheelbase version of the 200 series. With diesel engine, it is a respected and comfortable 'executive limousine', the sort of car used by many firms for such jobs as taking senior management to the airport.

The 600 limousine was a prestige eight-seater (above left and right). *Launched 1980, the Excalibur (left) was designed by Brooks Stevens after the Mercedes 500/540K of 1937-38, and has longer wheelbase. A Chevrolet V8 5-liter hides in the enormous engine compartment*

Interior of the 600 Limousine featuring optional television (above, top). In spite of the size of their cars, Daimler-Benz take energy conservation seriously, and evolved an aerodynamic shape for the second generation S-Class (above), launched September 1979. (Right): Special conversion of a 500SE by Panther Cars of Great Britain

Examples of the fascinating conversion work done by Panther Cars of Weybridge, Surrey, England, are seen on these pages. A 500SE gets a very traditional (and highly un-aerodynamic!) radiator grille (right, and below); and (facing page) an extravagant adaptation of 500SLC produces interior in white and red, and gull wing doors. (Lower right): Another luxury interior for a 500SE by Panther.

THE MARQUE OF ACHIEVEMENT

First you could hear the distant roar of the high performance 16 valve engine running at full bore; the noise increased rapidly as it approached. Then came the steadily rising scream of the tires. Finally the car itself was in view for a few seconds – long enough to note the completely different color of the front, black and red with the stains of millions of smashed insects. A sudden crescendo of noise as this ordinary Mercedes-Benz 190 saloon flashed by at over 150 mph. Then, almost as an anticlimax, it was gone, and another circuit of the high-speed bowl of the Nardo proving-ground in souther Italy was completed.

ested to the limit

went on like this for hour after hour, day and night, for
ore than a week. At the end of it, the three Mercedes
90E 16 valve saloons had broken three world speed and
stance records. This was a remarkable achievement of
gh-speed endurance in conditions of extreme
mperature, reaching 104°F (40°C) and rising to 120°F
0°C) inside the car.

For Daimler-Benz this adventure in the summer of 1983
as nothing new. The company has a long history of
cord-breaking and pioneering work setting the pace for
e world's cars. One of the earliest of such enterprises
ok place in America in 1895, when the *Times Herald*
fered $5000 cash prize for a race of 'horseless vehicles'
om Milwaukee to Chicago.

Oscar Mueller driving a Benz and Frank Duryea driving
car of his own make were the chief contenders. Other
competitors complained that they were not ready by race
day. Duryea crashed, leaving Mueller to win, covering the
92 mile course in just under 9½ hours. The main event had
been postponed to give competitors longer for preparation,
and this time Mueller was second, winning $1500. In the
same year six Daimler-powered cars were among the first
eight in the famous Paris-Bordeaux-Paris race, two of
them being Benz cars.

*Record-breaking 190E 16V at the Nardo
proving ground in southern Italy (left). The
last year up to start of World War I in 1914
produced this 117 racer (below, upper) and
saw Daimler win the GP of France and the
Vanderbilt race in America. (Lower): Another
Grand Prix car (1914) which has been
preserved and restored*

Postwar victories

A sizable book could be filled with the endless saga of Daimler-Benz racing victories through the years, including a series of triumphs when the company resumed racing in 1952. Less well remembered, perhaps, but still significant, was the catalog of international rally successes which Mercedes cars won in the late 1950s and early '60s.

During the notoriously testing Liège-Sofia-Liège rally of 1963, at a rally control in Yugoslavia, the marshal took a ruler and drew a line across his chart with the passing of every minute without arrival of any competitors. Suddenly the squat, purposeful shape of the Mercedes 230SL came

roaring into view and skidded to a halt in a cloud of dust. It was some minutes before anyone else came in, and the 230SL driven by Bohringer and Kaiser arrived back at Liège looking travel-stained but unmarked – a clear winner.

When the promising new Wankel rotary engine burst upon the motoring scene in the early 1960s, Daimler-Benz devoted immense effort to development of the new engine. They never put it into production, but its potential as a compact but powerful engine was illustrated by a special two-seater sports car, the C111. It appeared first with a three-rotor Wankel engine in 1969, and was then shown at Geneva in 1970 with a four-rotor Wankel, equivalent to a 4.8 liter conventional piston engine. The same special

ports car was later used to demonstrate speed and endurance for existing piston engines. A supercharged five-cylinder 3 liter diesel engine was fitted, which set new world records for diesel cars at the amazingly high speed of 157.4 mph for 10,000 miles.

Later, a Mark IV version of the legendary C111 was fitted with a V8 petrol engine with twin turbochargers, and achieved the fantastic speed of 403.9 km/h (251 mph).

The most extraordinary record of all was set by an aerodynamic Daimler-Benz economy special. This car managed 2875 miles per gallon of diesel fuel on the Hockenheimring motor-racing circuit.

The 1937 Type W125 Grand Prix car had eight cylinders in line in two batches of four, with four valves per cylinder. It was supercharged, and developed nearly 650 bhp from capacity of 5,660 c.c. (left and below). Caracciola won the European drivers' championship for the third year running in the W154 (bottom), which had a V12 3-liter engine with twin overhead camshafts for each bank of six cylinders, working four valves per cylinder – a total of 48 valves! It had twin superchargers and developed 450 bhp

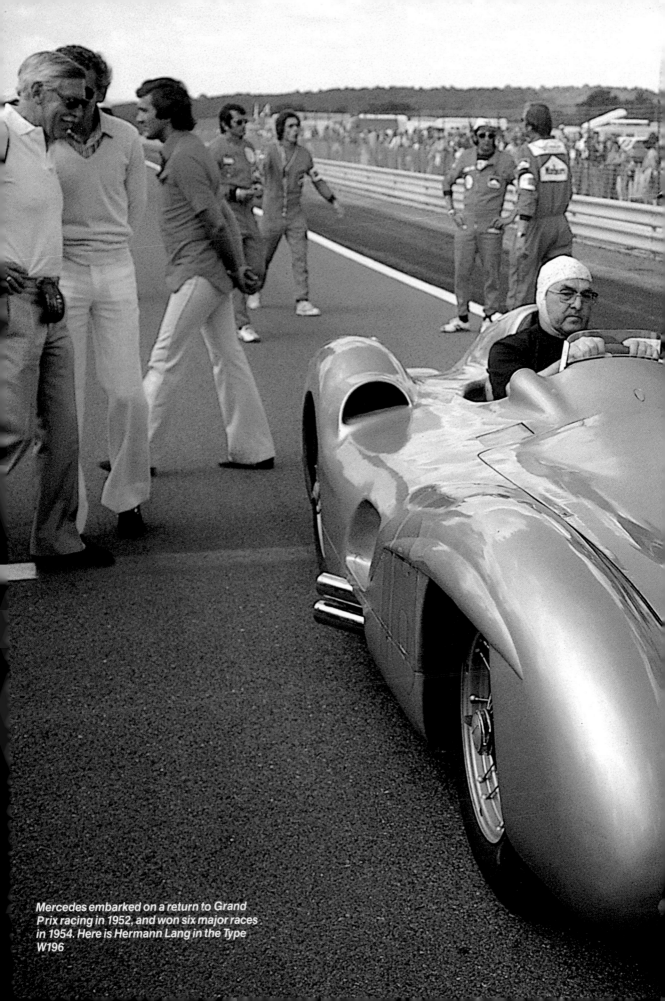

Mercedes embarked on a return to Grand Prix racing in 1952, and won six major races in 1954. Here is Hermann Lang in the Type W196

Phil Hill testing the W196 unstreamlined version at the Nürburgring (left). A 1955 300SL took part in the 1984 Mille Miglia commemoration event, recalling its win with Stirling Moss and journalist Denis Jenkinson (above)

One of the most famous experimental cars in the world was the Mercedes-Benz C111 two-seater with gull wing doors. It started life as a test-bed for the Wankel rotary engine, built under license from NSU, who held the Wankel patents. First shown at the 1969 Frankfurt Show, it had a three-rotor engine, but later a four-rotor Wankel, equivalent to 4.8 liters, was installed in 1972. Eventually the Wankel engine was dropped, and the C111 was used to set many records with a diesel engine

First launched as the 230SL, the second generation SL was later available with 2.5- and 2.8-liter six-cylinder engines

*Back endpaper
500SE, modified in 1981 for improved economy by raising the gear ratios and developing engines to give high torque at low rpm*

Picture Credits

Bicton Hall of Transport 9 bottom **Stuart Bladon** 50-51 **Neill Bruce Photographic** 36-37, 39, 40-41, 42 bottom, 44-45 **Daimler-Benz** back cover, 9 top & centre, 12 top, 24 bottom, 28-29, 29 bottom, 32 top, 37 bottom, 46-47, 55 top, 57 bottom, back endpaper **Mirco Decet** title page, 12 bottom, 38-39, 45 top, 35 bottom, 49, 50 top, 52 & 53, 61, 46 **Geoffrey Goddard** 58-59, 63 (inset), 60-61 **Chris Harvey** 38 **Mercedes Benz UK** 50 bottom, 54-55 **Midland Motor Museum,**

Bridgenorth 16-17 **Andrew Morland** front endpaper, 24 top, 30-31 top, 24-25 top, 29 top, 32 bottom, 35 top, 37 top, 55 bottom, 64 **National Motor Museum** 48-49 bottom **The Photo Source** 4-5, 10-11, 26-27, 42-43 top **Peter Roberts Collection** front cover, half-title page. 7, 15, 18-19 bottom, 20-21, 22-23, 30-31 bottom, 32 centre, 42-43 bottom, 56-57, 62-63 **Tony Stone Associates** 6-7, 8-9, 12-13, 14-15, 18, 24-25 bottom, 42 top. 57 top **Nicky Wright** 31, 32-33, 45 bottom **ZEFA** 18-19 top, 30, 63 (inset)